The Children's Bible Atlas has been created and produced by
HarperCollinsPublishers Limited
77-85 Fulham Palace Road, London W6 8JB

©HarperCollinPublishers Limited
©*Text* Henry Wansbrough
©*Maps* Times Books Limited

Photographs ©Henry Wansbrough
pp 8,9,10,13,14,15,17,18 (top)23,28,29.
30,31,32,33,34,35,36 (top/bottom)

Other Photographs ©HarperCollinsPublishers Limited

Design Schermuly Design Co. London.

All rights reserved

First published in Great Britain in 1997

ISBN 000197967-1

CHILDREN'S
ATLAS OF THE BIBLE

A photographic account of the journeys in the Bible from Abraham to St. Paul

Henry Wansbrough

HarperCollins*Publishers*

Contents

Introduction

This book shows you the lands in which the events of the Bible happened. Most of these events took place on a narrow strip of land beside the Mediterranean Sea. This strip of land, only fifty miles across, has had several names, first Canaan, then Palestine, and now the Land of Israel. It is a land of sharp contrasts. There are rocky hills where vines still grow. There are sandy deserts where nothing grows. There are little rivers whose water produces rich vegetation. It is often called the Holy Land because it is the land of the Bible.

The first man called by God was Abraham. He came into the Holy Land by walking, from what we now call the Persian Gulf, up the fertile river valley to the north and finally across a desert to Canaan. At the end of the Bible, Paul travelled from Canaan, which was by then called Palestine, taking the message of the New Testament all the way west to Rome.

In the two thousand years of history which is told in the Bible, the land was fought over by the armies of several great empires. The different maps show you the places which were important at each stage of the story. You can see the routes people took in their journeys over the desert, beside the rivers and across the sea. The pictures try to give you an impression of how people and things looked at the time. All this should help you to follow the stories and imagine what it felt like to be there at that time.

Henry Wansbrough

Ur and Mesopotamia

Abraham was the first leader of the Hebrews. He lived with his family in Mesopotamia, the fertile land between two great rivers, the Tigris and the Euphrates. Each spring the rivers flood the land around. This water combines with the hot sun of summer to make a huge expanse of rich cornland. This produces more than enough grain for everyone and leaves some people free to work at other skills.

Abraham lived in the city of Ur, in the marshes near the mouth of the River Euphrates. It was a busy port. Timber and metal were brought down from cities higher up the Euphrates. At Ur merchants loaded these onto sea-going ships, and exchanged them for cargoes of precious stones, pearls, spices and ivory. It became important to keep records and send letters, so writing was developed by scribes. They wrote by making impressions with a sharp wedge-shaped stick in damp clay tablets.

Many little statues of gold and jade made by the people of Ur have been recovered. Numerous treasures have also been found in the graves of the kings and queens of Ur. It was

The brick ruins of a ziggurat overlooking the flat plain of Borsippa in Mesopotamia.

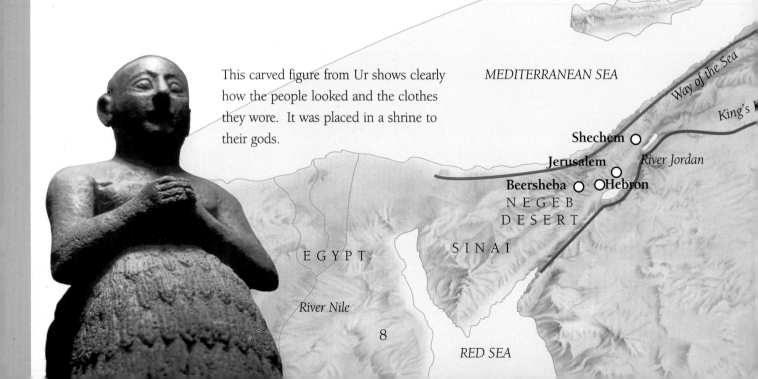

This carved figure from Ur shows clearly how the people looked and the clothes they wore. It was placed in a shrine to their gods.

MEDITERRANEAN SEA

Way of the Sea

King's

Shechem ○

Jerusalem ○

River Jordan

Beersheba ○ ○Hebron

NEGEB
DESERT

EGYPT

SINAI

River Nile

RED SEA

8

thought that the monarchs would need servants in the after-life and so slaves were slaughtered and buried with their masters. One grave even contained a complete team of horses, harnessed and ready to draw the dead king's chariot.

The Mesopotamians worshipped the sun, moon and stars. As temples they built huge brick pyramids in steps, called ziggurats. The top of the ziggurat would have been an ideal place to watch the moon and stars. They could calculate eclipses of the sun and moon. The modern system of sixty seconds in a minute, sixty minutes in an hour and twenty-four hours in a day comes from this ancient system.

A decorated harp in the shape of a boat from the royal graves at Ur.

The map below shows the two main trade routes, the King's Highway and the Way of the Sea which connected Ur to the southern Mediterranean.

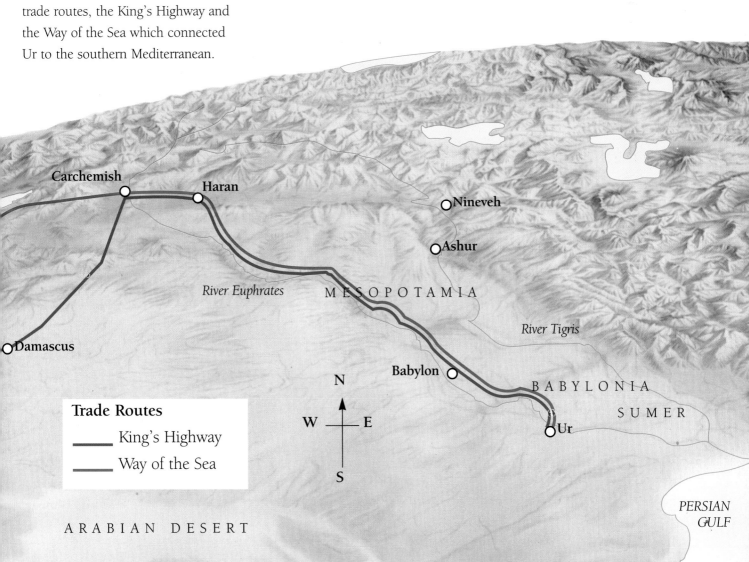

Carchemish
Haran
Nineveh
Ashur
River Euphrates
MESOPOTAMIA
River Tigris
Damascus
Babylon
BABYLONIA
SUMER
N
W — E
S
Ur

Trade Routes
—— King's Highway
—— Way of the Sea

ARABIAN DESERT

PERSIAN GULF

Abraham's wanderings on the edge of civilisation

A nomadic mother carries her baby on her back.

Haran was a fine city at the crossroads of several trading routes in northern Mesopotamia. Abraham was living there with his family when God told him to travel south to the land of Canaan. Abraham and his wife, Sarah, had no children of their own, but God promised Abraham that one day his descendants would be as many as the grains of sand on the seashore or the stars in the sky.

Abraham obeyed God and went to Canaan with his family and flocks. Canaan is the land bordered on one side by the valley of the River Jordan, which flows into the Dead Sea, and on the other side by the Mediterranean Sea. Abraham travelled in the rough mountainous land, away from the few large towns and the fertile Jordan valley. He and his followers lived in tents and moved from one place to another to find grass for their sheep to eat. They were nomads, and carried everything they owned with them. When there was a drought they

This donkey is carrying all the possessions of a modern nomadic family.

MEDITERRANEAN SEA

Tyre ○
Hazor ○

C A N A A N

Shechem ○
Jerusalem ○ ○Jericho   *River Jordan*
Beersheba ○ ○ ○ *DEAD SEA*
Hebron
E G Y P T   N E G E B
D E S E R T

walked south to Egypt, just as nomads still do today. The great River Nile flows through Egypt, so there is always plenty of water.

When Abraham and Sarah were very old they had a son, Isaac. When Sarah died, Abraham bought a cave at Hebron for her burial. It became the tribal centre where every year they would all gather. Isaac wandered in the area of Beersheba on the edge of the desert. There he began to plant crops. When Isaac was old enough to get married, his father found him a wife from among their relations back in Haran. Isaac's son Jacob himself had twelve sons. There was not enough pasture round Beersheba, and they sometimes had to look for grazing as far away as Shechem in the north.

The map shows the route of Abraham and his followers from his birthplace in Ur to Egypt, where he fled from the drought in Canaan.

The wedding feast of Abraham's grandson Jacob. Both Isaac and Jacob returned north to Haran to find brides from their own clan.

Abraham lived as a nomad. All strangers were welcome. Food and water were always shared.

ARABIAN DESERT

11

Joseph in Egypt

Jacob was the leader of the Hebrews after Abraham and Isaac. He had twelve sons. Joseph was the youngest and his father loved him best. Joseph's elder brothers came to hate him. They thought him spoilt and cheeky – and so he was. One day they sold him to slave merchants who were travelling south to Egypt. They told their father that a wild beast had eaten him.

These pyramids near Heliopolis were tombs for the ancient Kings of Egypt. They were built before the Hebrews arrived in Egypt.

The king of Egypt was all-powerful. Egypt was controlled through ranks of officials who kept watch on each other.

Joseph was sold as a slave to an Egyptian official. However when the Egyptian king was worried by a dream he had had, Joseph found he was able to explain it. The king rewarded him by putting him in charge of all Egypt's food stores. He became an important official.

The kings of Egypt were rich, their palaces were beautiful and large. The Egyptians made a written record of everything from the name of the king to the number of bags of grain stored in his granary. They also made vivid pictures of every-day life, such as dancing, feasting, hunting and working.

One year there was a drought in Canaan, and Joseph's brothers went down to Egypt looking for grain. They went straight to the man in charge of the food supplies but did not recognise Joseph. Joseph's revenge was to tease them before revealing himself as their brother. Then he arranged for Jacob and the rest of the Hebrews to join him in Egypt. The Hebrews settled here for four hundred years. In time the Egyptians came to treat the Hebrews as slaves. The Hebrews longed to be free to return to the land God had promised to Abraham.

A caravan of donkeys carry heavy bags of grain after the harvest.

12

SEA OF GALILEE

MEDITERRANEAN
SEA

CANAAN

River Jordan

Jerusalem○

DEAD SEA

Joseph grew up in Canaan but was taken
south-west, to Egypt, where he eventually
became rich and powerful, (see map below).

N E G E B
D E S E R T

A R A B A H

N
W┼E
S

Nile Delta

○ **Heliopolis**

River Nile

S I N A I

RED SEA

E G Y P T

○ **Karnak**
○ **Luxor**

13

Exodus

A wall painting of an Egyptian official beating a servant. Slaves were punished with more brutality.

The hills of eastern Sinai on the route taken by the Israelites towards the Promised Land.

Eventually the Hebrews escaped from Egypt and, led by Moses, they headed for the desert of Sinai. This is an expanse of dry sand with mountains of bare rock. It looks as though a giant has emptied huge barrow-loads of rocks onto the bare sand. There is no soil or vegetation anywhere.

Near the coast of Sinai are copper mines. Lettering scratched on the rock shows that Hebrew slaves once worked there. Moses and his people returned to these places they already knew. Egyptian forces pursued them, but were drowned when their chariots were swamped with the sea water on the path taken by the fleeing Hebrews. No one today knows where this happened along the route of the Exodus.

In the barren desert the Hebrews wandered with their flocks for forty years. They got hungry and complained to Moses. God sent them manna, which was like bread and quails (small birds) to eat. In their sulky bad temper the Hebrews melted down their jewelery, made a gold statue of a bull and danced round it. When Moses found out he made them grind this golden calf to powder.

It was in Sinai that the Hebrews felt God calling them to be his special chosen people. God gave Moses the Law to shape his people of Israel. Obedience to the Law sealed the bond between them. The Law was preserved in a sacred box, the Ark of the Covenant. As the people wandered over Sinai, they carried the Ark of the Covenant with them. Other tribes joined them and they grew into a strong and warlike nation, the Israelites.

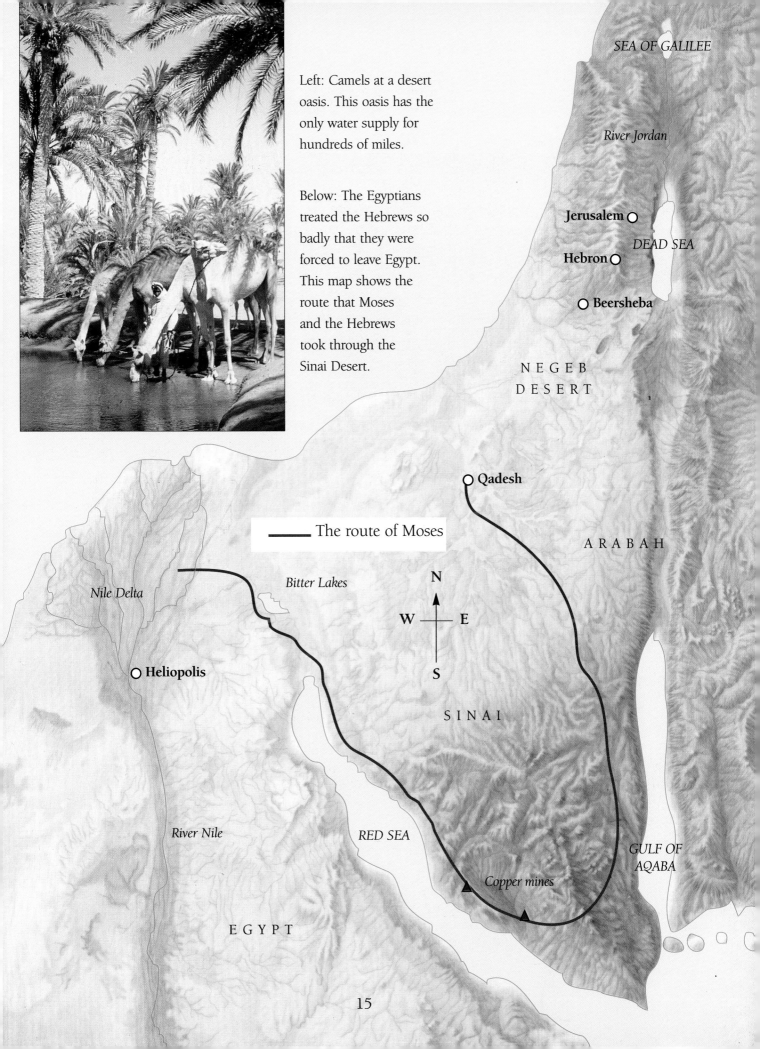

Left: Camels at a desert oasis. This oasis has the only water supply for hundreds of miles.

Below: The Egyptians treated the Hebrews so badly that they were forced to leave Egypt. This map shows the route that Moses and the Hebrews took through the Sinai Desert.

SEA OF GALILEE

River Jordan

Jerusalem ○

DEAD SEA

Hebron ○

○ **Beersheba**

N E G E B
D E S E R T

○ **Qadesh**

—— The route of Moses

A R A B A H

N
W — E
S

Nile Delta

Bitter Lakes

○ **Heliopolis**

S I N A I

River Nile

RED SEA

GULF OF
AQABA

Copper mines

E G Y P T

15

Israel and the Philistines

The Israelites came into the land of Canaan from the east, across the River Jordan. There were already great cities in the land, fortresses of the Egyptians, who had ruled the land for centuries. Two of these are at Megiddo and Beth Shean which guard the trade-routes from Mesopotamia to Egypt. Other great cities, like Jerusalem in the hills of central Canaan, were the strongholds of a tribe called the Jebusites. At first the Israelites settled only in the chain of hills which form a backbone along the length of central Canaan. This was stony ground, difficult to plough for corn. Instead, the Israelites planted grape vines and olive trees, which grow well in these dry conditions.

Soon after the Israelites arrived, the Philistines settled on the rich coastal plain near the Mediterranean Sea, where Jaffa oranges now grow. They quickly established a number of strong cities. The name 'Philistia' became Palestine, meaning 'the land of the Philistines'. The Philistines grew more and more powerful, and often invaded the hill-country. The Israelites built a line of

The Israelites used small curved hunting bows and arrows and long hunting daggers to defend themselves against their enemies.

fortresses along the foothills to try to keep them out, but the Philistines had better weapons than the Israelites. They also used chariots in battle, much as tanks are used today. They even captured the Ark of the Covenant, which the Israelites had brought with them from the desert as the sign of God's presence among them.

The Israelites were weak because they had no central government. Each of the tribes had its own territory and tried to guard that, but would not willingly help another tribe. The Philistines were so menacing that, in the end, several of the Israelite tribes united to make Saul their king. Then the champion of the Philistines, a huge man called Goliath, challenged the Israelites to settle their war by arranging to fight in single combat. A young shepherd called David felled Goliath with a single stone from his sling and then cut off his head. The Philistine army fled.

The map shows the cities held by the Israelites, the Philistines and the Egyptians. The Israelites and the Philistines often fought each other in war and several cities changed hands during the battles.

SYRIA

SEA OF GALILEE

▲ Megiddo

Beth Shean ▲

River Jordan

▲ Taanach

CANAAN

✡ Shiloh

✡ Shechem

■ Joppe

✡ Bethel

Jericho ✡

○ Gezer

○ Jerusalem

PHILISTIA

■ Ashdod

■ Ekron

○ Beth Shemesh

DEAD SEA

■ Ashqelon

✡ Hebron

■ Gath

○ Lachish

▲ Gaza

N

W — E

S

▲ Egyptian fortress towns

■ Philistine towns

✡ Israelite towns

○ Towns that changed hands

A watch-tower in Canaan.

David's Kingdom

The Ark of the Covenant as it was pictured in this stone carving at Capernaum. It is one of the very few known pictures of the Ark.

A procession of musicians. King David was a musician and a poet. His psalms are still sung today.

The Israelites settled in two separate groups. The northern tribes formed the nation of Israel, with Saul as their king. The southern tribes occupied an area from the Dead Sea to the Negeb desert, known as Judah. Saul became jealous of David's popularity and tried to drive him away. David hid in the caves near En Gedi. But when Saul was killed in battle and his surviving son turned out to be worthless as a leader, the northerners accepted David as their king too. He was married to Saul's daughter, Michal, and did his best to unite the two parts of his kingdom.

With his private army David captured Jerusalem. Joab, his courageous general, climbed up through the pipe which supplied the city with water. He crawled with his men to the inside of the city and took it by surprise. At that time Jerusalem was on the frontier between Israel and Judah, so it made an ideal capital city for King David. David found the Ark of the Covenant, the symbol of God's presence among his people, and bought it to Jerusalem with great ceremony. So the city became the religious centre for all the Israelites.

David was successful in all his wars. He captured many of the cities that the Israelites had been unable to conquer. The territory finally won by David was greater than Israel had ever possessed, either before or since.

Above: King David brought the Ark to Jerusalem with rejoicing. His wife despised him for dancing in front of his people.

Right: A cross-section of the hill on which Jerusalem was built, showing the water course which provided a way for Joab and his men to crawl, unseen, into Jerusalem.

Hazor ○

SEA OF GALILEE

N
W — E
S

○ Megiddo

River Jordan

I S R A E L

Jericho ○

○ Jerusalem

○ Beth Shemesh

Hebron ○

En Gedi ○   *DEAD SEA*

J U D A H

N E G E B
D E S E R T

This map shows Israel and Judah, the lands in
which the two Israelite groups settled. David
captured Jerusalem and in doing so united the
two kindoms into one great Israelite nation.

19

Solomon's Jerusalem

Solomon became king of Israel after the death of his father David. His father had made Israel great by war. Solomon kept Israel rich by trade. All the trade between the Mediterranean Sea, Central Asia, Africa and Anatolia, (the area we know as Turkey), passed through some part of his kingdom. He sold horses from Anatolia to Egypt and chariots from Egypt to Anatolia. He opened up the copper mines in the southern desert at Timnah. He had a fleet of ships at Elath on the Red Sea which imported gold, ivory and apes from Africa.

Solomon used his wealth to make Jerusalem a royal city. He built a great Temple to God which was panelled entirely with precious cedar wood inlaid with gold. Two cherubim, winged figures of carved olive wood, covered with gold, stood on either side of the Ark of the Covenant in the most holy room in the Temple. He also built a royal palace and a walled stronghold or citadel. The houses of the ordinary people were

The first great Temple in Jerusalem was built by Solomon.

Below: A modern reconstruction of Jerusalem at the time of Solomon. This was twice the size of the city he inherited from David. A few remains from Solomon's city can be seen in modern Jerusalem.

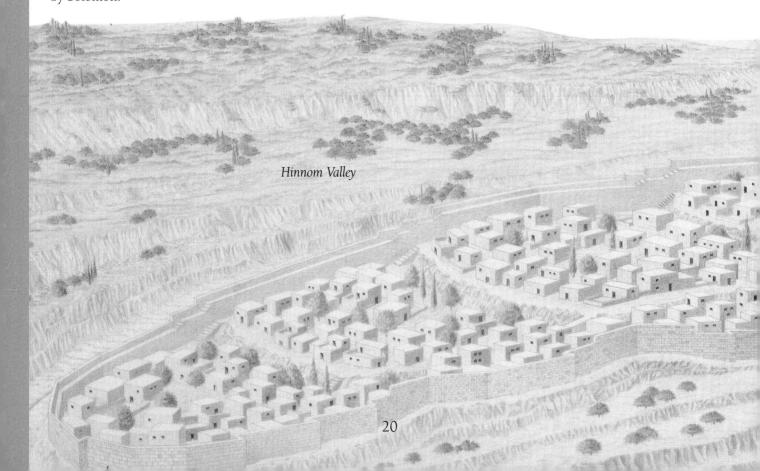

Hinnom Valley

below the citadel. The city was now more than twice as big as David's city had been.

Solomon also rebuilt and fortified the cities to the north, like Hazor and Megiddo, and stabled his horses and chariots there. He protected the trade route across the desert to the east and made it safe. He also built the city of Palmyra as a half-way point for the camel-trains.

He married seven hundred women. Many were the daughters of neighbouring kings, and this strengthened his links to foreign countries. But Solomon's foreign wives brought with them foreign religions and statues as rivals to the God of Israel. Solomon favoured his own tribal area of Judah to the south. Those to the north, in Israel, were forced to provide free labour for a long period each year. They had to work in the mines and to build the cities. This kept them away from their homes and families for months on end and they became bitter and rebellious.

Solomon was famous for his wealth. He was also valued for his wisdom. Wise men were revered because they shared in God's own wisdom.

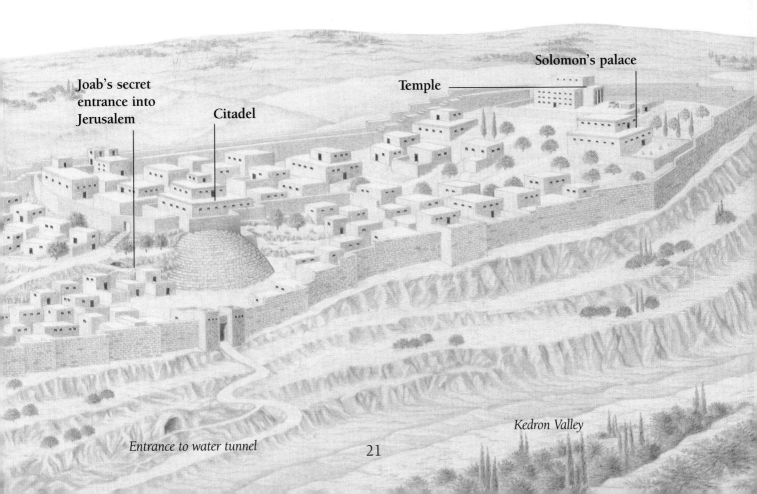

Joab's secret entrance into Jerusalem

Citadel

Temple

Solomon's palace

Kedron Valley

Entrance to water tunnel

21

Israel and Judah Separate

Solomon was king of Israel at a time when the great empires of Mesopotamia to the east and Egypt to the south were unusually peaceful. Solomon's son Rehoboam came to the throne when these great foreign states were ruled by more aggressive emperors. In his own kingdom Rehoboam mistreated his northern people and they quickly rebelled. Israel split off from Judah and chose a new king, Jeroboam. A new centre of worship was set up at Bethel, a rival to the Temple in Jerusalem. Frequent wars between Israel and Judah followed and much of the land conquered by David was lost to groups of people who broke away and set up their own kings.

The prophet Ahijah tore his cloak into twelve pieces. He gave ten pieces to Jeroboam to show him how many tribes in Israel would follow him.

The Egyptian army invaded Judah from the south and plundered many fine cities, including Jerusalem. However, David's family remained the royal family of Judah for another three hundred and fifty years.

In Israel, one after another of the kings was assassinated. Zimri was king for only seven days. Samaria became the capital city. The northern kings were more interested in making money by trade than in loyalty to God. They married the daughters of neighbouring royal families to strengthen friendship between them. King Ahab married Jezebel, daughter of the priest-king of Tyre. Jezebel led Ahab into the worship of Baal, the local god of thunder and lightning. Elijah, and the other prophets told the king and his people that disaster would follow if they deserted the God of Israel. The king was afraid of Elijah, but still did not follow his advice.

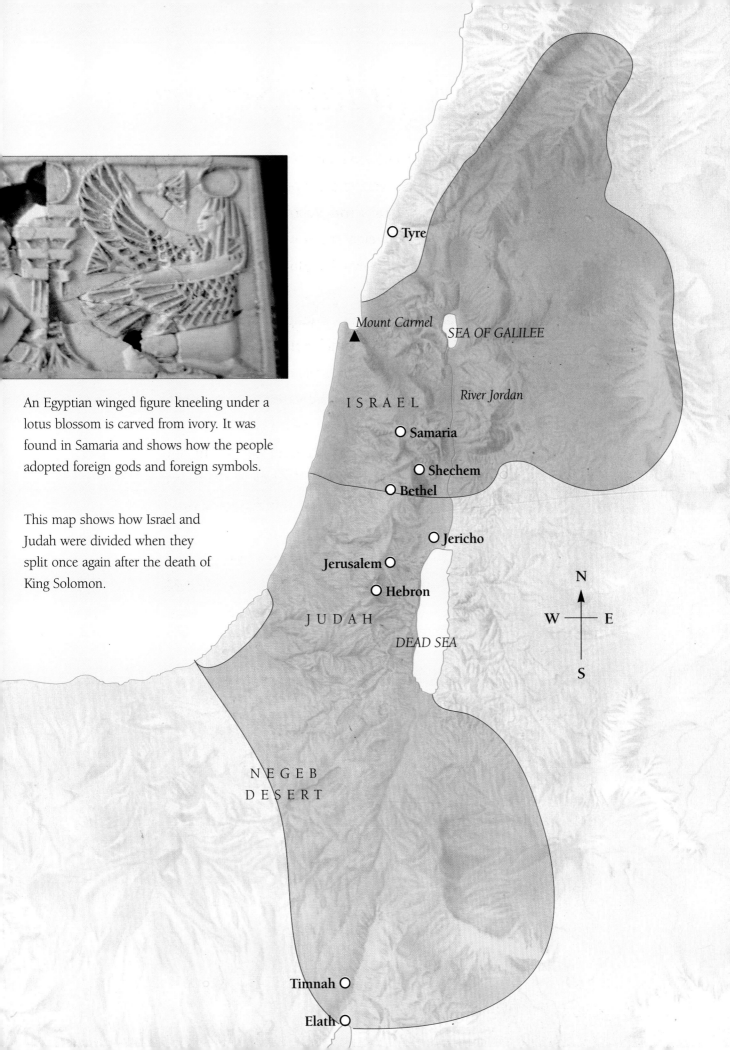

An Egyptian winged figure kneeling under a lotus blossom is carved from ivory. It was found in Samaria and shows how the people adopted foreign gods and foreign symbols.

This map shows how Israel and Judah were divided when they split once again after the death of King Solomon.

O Tyre

Mount Carmel
▲

SEA OF GALILEE

I S R A E L   *River Jordan*

O Samaria

O Shechem

O Bethel

O Jericho

Jerusalem O

O Hebron

J U D A H

DEAD SEA

N
W ← → E
S

N E G E B
D E S E R T

Timnah O

Elath O

The Assyrian Empire

During the last seven centuries before Christ five great empires dominated Israel, Judah and Palestine. The first empire developed from the ancient kingdom of Assyria, a nation which had grown wealthy on the fertile plain between the Tigris and Euphrates rivers. The King of Assyria claimed to be king of the world. The kings were careful rulers and recorded their laws on clay tablets stored in great libraries. These records often give an Assyrian version of events that are also described in the Bible, including the creation of the world and the great flood. The Assyrians had huge stone statues carved of their kings, especially fighting wars. They show men with strong faces and square-cut beards, carefully curled.

Right: The Assyrian soldiers carry the heads of enemy soldiers slaughtered in battle. There are many carvings celebrating Assyria's brutal conquests.

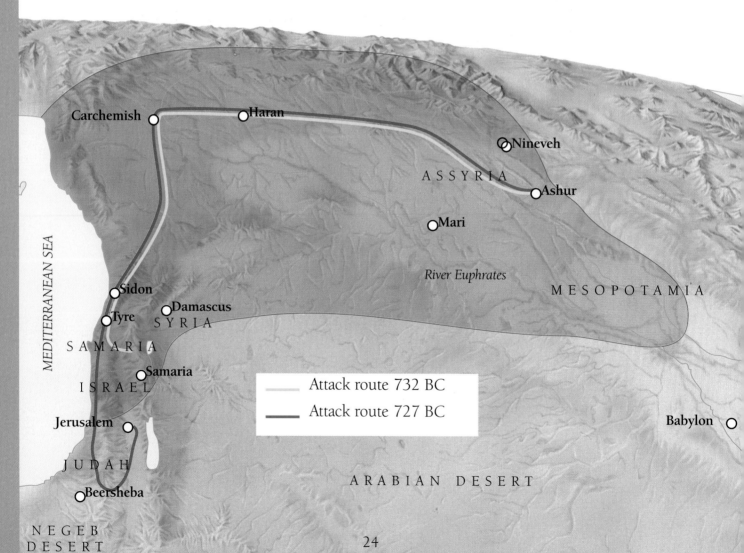

MEDITERRANEAN SEA

Carchemish

Haran

Nineveh

ASSYRIA

Ashur

Mari

River Euphrates

MESOPOTAMIA

Sidon

Damascus

Tyre

SYRIA

SAMARIA

Samaria

ISRAEL

Jerusalem

JUDAH

Beersheba

NEGEB DESERT

ARABIAN DESERT

Babylon

Attack route 732 BC
Attack route 727 BC

The Assyrians came across the River Euphrates at Carchemish, turned south and conquered Damascus and most of Israel, except the capital Samaria. Its king, Jehu, had to pay them tribute. The Assyrian royal records claim that the King of Assyria 'overwhelmed like a snowstorm' the King of Judah, who then 'fled like a bird'. So Israel came to be ruled by Assyria, but Judah further south escaped.

In 727 BC the Assyrian king died and Israel rebelled. The new Assyrian king attacked and destroyed Samaria. All the people of Samaria were massacred or roped together, secured with meat hooks and marched off across the desert to Assyria. In Assyria they worked as slaves, building huge palaces and temples.

Twenty years later the Assyrian army attacked many cities in Judah. They even threatened Jerusalem and their armies beseiged it 'like a bird in a cage', as the Assyrian records say. King Hezekiah bribed the Assyrians to spare his city, Jerusalem, giving them quantities of gold and silver. Hezekiah even stripped some of it from the Temple itself.

The map shows the routes taken by the invading Assyrian forces which attacked and conquered many parts of Israel, Judah and Samaria.

CASPIAN SEA

N

W ——|—— E

S

iver Tigris

BABYLONIA

SUMER

◯Ur

The Babylonians

Right: In Babylon beside the Euphrates the Israelites worshipped God and prayed to be delivered from captivity.

Below: The map shows the attack routes that the Babylonians took when they captured Gaza and Jerusalem.

Babylon was a great city about one hundred miles south of Assyria on the River Euphrates. When the Assyrian empire grew weak it was overwhelmed and divided up between the Medes in the north and the King of Babylon. The Babylonians built an empire greater than that of the Assyrians. They protected their land, especially their trade routes. Rebellion led to slaughter or enslavement of whole nations.

In 609BC the Babylonians totally destroyed the Egyptian army at Gaza on the border of Egypt, which now became part of the Babylonian empire. In the north, the Babylonians ruled up to the River Halys in Anatolia, modern Turkey.

The King of Judah, Jehoiakim, rebelled. So Jerusalem was

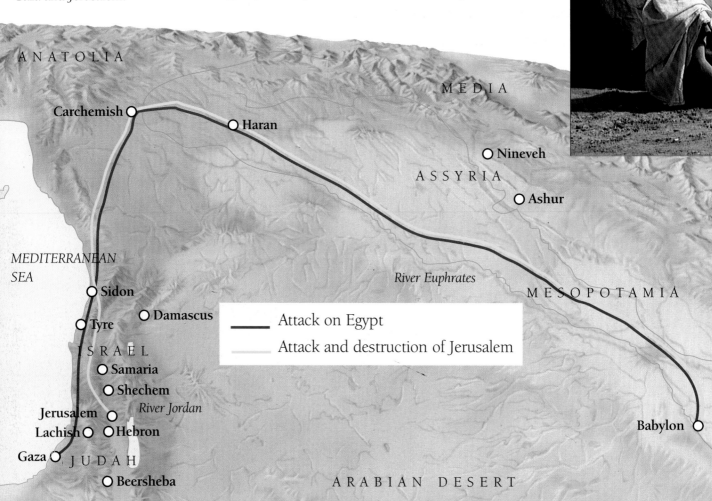

ANATOLIA

MEDIA

Carchemish

Haran

Nineveh

ASSYRIA

Ashur

MEDITERRANEAN SEA

River Euphrates

MESOPOTAMIA

Sidon

Damascus

Tyre

ISRAEL

Samaria

Shechem

River Jordan

Jerusalem

Lachish　Hebron

Gaza　JUDAH

Babylon

Beersheba

ARABIAN DESERT

NEGEB DESERT

▬▬▬	Attack on Egypt
▬▬▬	Attack and destruction of Jerusalem

besieged and defeated in 597BC. Jehoiakim and the nobles, priests, weapon makers and the treasure of the Temple were taken to Babylon. A sad relic was found on clay tablets – the account books for the meals of King Jehoiakim and his family, prisoners at the King of Babylon's table for thirty-seven years.

The Bible tells the religious history of this time and records the warnings of the prophet Jeremiah. He told all the people left in Judah that their strength was to be found in the faithful worship of God. The people of Jerusalem failed God and rebelled against Nebuchadnezzar, King of Babylon. In 587BC the city was attacked, defeated and burned. The King was forced to watch while his children were killed. Then he was blinded; this was the end of the line of kings from David. Thousands of Judeans were taken as slaves across the desert to Babylon. The Bible says, "On the rivers of Babylon, there we sat and wept as we remembered Jerusalem."

Babylonian soldiers recorded the number of the enemy slaughtered by countirg their severed heads.

CASPIAN SEA

N
W — E
S

River Tigris

BABYLONIA

SUMER

O Ur

The Persian Empire

In 539BC Babylon itself was captured from the north by Cyrus the Persian. Cyrus had first defeated the Median empire in the north. The Persian Empire became even larger than the Babylonian Empire. The Persians controlled this vast area by allowing local kings to remain on their thrones if they paid tribute, did as they were told, and did not make or join in any war against Persia. Only the Greeks fought off the Persian army, stopping their advance west at the Aegean sea.

Cyrus allowed the Jewish exiles in Babylon to return to Jerusalem. Many had become bankers and merchants and preferred to stay in Babylon. About fifty thousand of them returned to Judah and began to rebuild the walls and all the buildings that had been destroyed in Jerusalem. They built a new, smaller Temple. Cyrus sent back the gold and silver which had been taken from the Temple by the Babylonians. They were often attacked by local people, so they worked with their weapons in their hands, ready to defend themselves. Building in these conditions was very slow.

The capital of the Persian empire was at Persepolis. Carvings on the palace staircase there show many different peoples bringing gifts from their own countries to the king. The Persians worshipped Ahura-Mazda, a god of the sun, but Cyrus also asked the Jews to pray and offer sacrifices for him in their Temple.

The palace at Persepolis was huge. It served as a royal house, administrative centre, citadel, treasury, barracks for soldiers, horses and chariots.

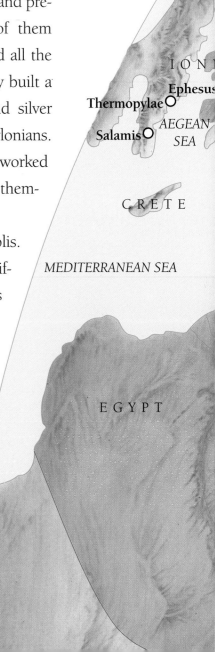

ION

Ephesus

Thermopylae O

AEGEAN

Salamis O   SEA

CRETE

MEDITERRANEAN SEA

EGYPT

The map shows the extent of the vast and powerful Persian Empire which was controlled from its capital at Persepolis.

CASPIAN SEA

BLACK SEA

MEDIA

PERSIA

○ Byzantium

DIA

○ Salamis

YPRUS

○ Sidon

○ Tyre   ○ Damascus

SEA OF GALILEE

○ Babylon

○ Persepolis

A Persian soldier on
guard forever as a
carved decoration on
a stairway in the
palace at Persepolis.

○ Jerusalem
○ Gaza *DEAD SEA*
UDAH

N
W ─┼─ E
S

PERSIAN GULF

ARABIAN
DESERT

RED SEA

An extraordinary,
double-headed griffin,
a mythical Persian
beast that guarded
gold treasure.

Alexander the Great

In 334BC Alexander of Macedon led his army from Greece into Asia. In twelve astonishing years he conquered the lands of Persia, Babylon, Mesopotamia, Syria, Israel, Judah, Palestine and Egypt. His army finally stopped in the Hindu Kush and on the Indus river in northern India. In many places he built cities named "Alexandria" after himself. He considered all the people of his empire to be equals and tried to make them think of each other as brothers. Everywhere people spoke Greek, took on Greek customs and learnt Greek philosophy. At Alexandria in Egypt there was such a big colony of Greek-speaking Jews that the Bible was translated from Hebrew into Greek for them. It was also at this time that some books in Greek were added to the Bible. Greek theatres, athletic tracks and temples were built even in Palestine.

After Alexander's death his empire was left to his Macedonian generals and finally split into three kingdoms. In Egypt the Ptolemy family ruled and in Syria the Seleucids were kings. Fighting was constant between Egypt and Syria. For almost one hundred years their soldiers marched backwards and forwards through Palestine until the Syrian king, Antiochus III captured Judah. Later when the Syrian king needed money to pay for his war against Rome he made his Jewish subjects pay huge taxes. At the same time he tried to make the Jews give up their special customs and become like all the other people in his kingdom and worship Greek gods. Many Jews refused and were prepared to die for their faith. The Maccabees led some of the most successful of the revolts by the Jews who finally cleared the Syrians out of Jerusalem.

The ruins of the Parthenon and the other famous Greek temples on the Acropolis, the rocky hill above Athens.

This map shows the extent of the Greek Empire following Alexander's many successful campaigns.

MACEDO

GREECE
Pella
Ephesus
Thermopylae
Athens   AEGEAN
          SEA

CRETE

MEDITERRANEAN SEA

Alexandria

EGYPT

Philadelphi.

River Nile

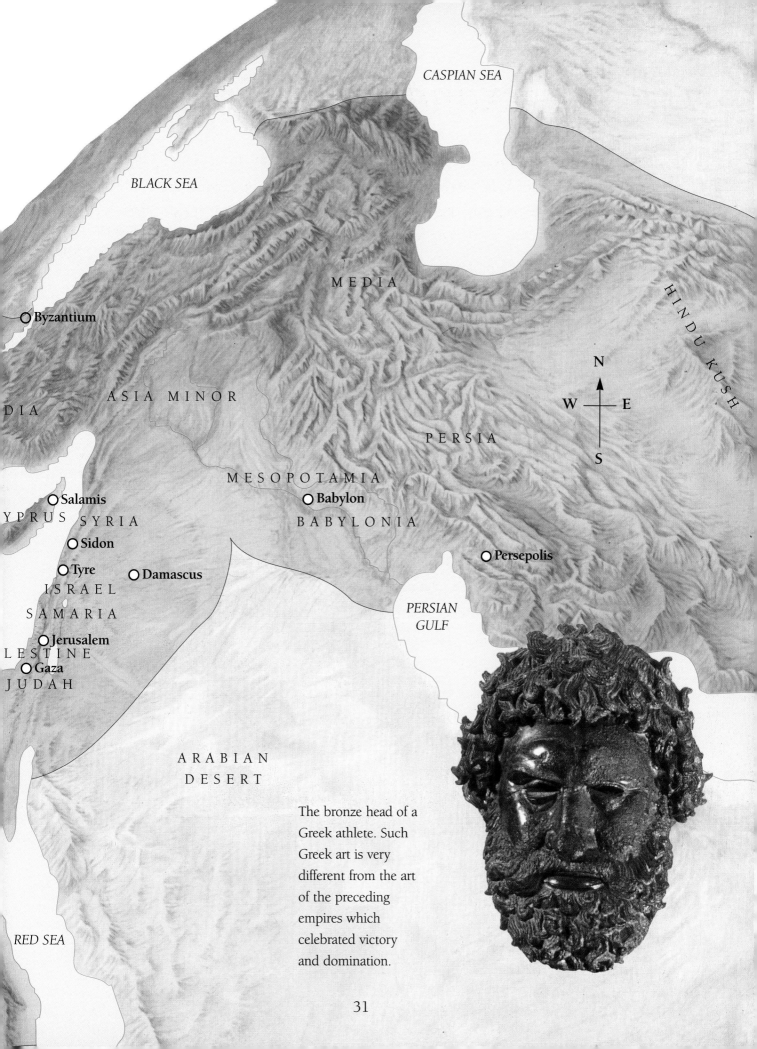

CASPIAN SEA

BLACK SEA

MEDIA

HINDU KUSH

○ Byzantium

N
W ← → E
S

ASIA MINOR

DIA

PERSIA

MESOPOTAMIA

YPRUS ○ Salamis ○ Babylon

SYRIA BABYLONIA

○ Sidon ○ Persepolis

○ Tyre ○ Damascus

ISRAEL

SAMARIA PERSIAN GULF

○ Jerusalem

LESTINE

○ Gaza

JUDAH

ARABIAN DESERT

The bronze head of a
Greek athlete. Such
Greek art is very
different from the art
of the preceding
empires which
celebrated victory
and domination.

RED SEA

31

The Romans and Herod

The Maccabees eventually won freedom from the Syrian king for Jerusalem, Judah and Idumea, the land to the south. Then they conquered land in Samaria and Galilee to the north and some land to the east of the Jordan. The Hasmonean family descended from the Maccabees set themselves up as a royal family, controlling the Temple in Jerusalem. Civil war broke out between families with rival claims to the priesthood. Some men set up their own community in isolation at Qumran beside the Dead Sea.

The Roman Empire included all the land around the Mediterranean Sea and extended as far as Britain to the west. By 64BC the great Roman general Pompey had conquered Syria to the east. The Hasmoneans and the priestly families in Judah, asked Pompey to decide which of them should rule the whole area. His solution was to bring Galilee, Judah and Idumaea under Roman rule. The food-supplies for Pompey's army were managed by an Idumaean, Antipater, and Pompey made him the ruler of Galilee.

Antipater's son, Herod, became king of the whole of the remaining Jewish nation. Herod's mother was a Jew, but he had grown up in Rome and was a childhood friend of the Roman

The port of Caesarea first built by Herod, was the chief port of the Eastern Mediterranean until recently. Roman remains can still be seen clearly today.

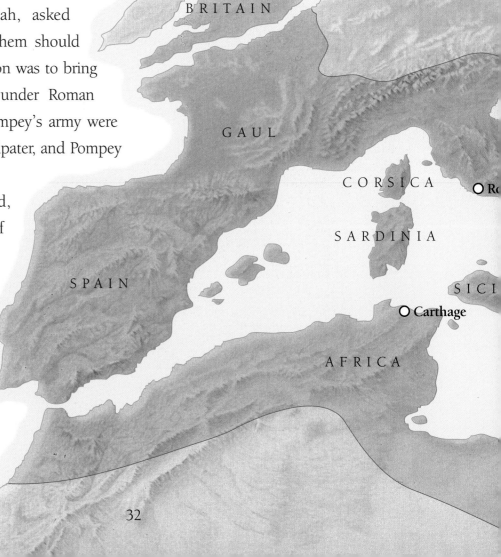

BRITAIN

GAUL

CORSICA

Ro

SARDINIA

SPAIN

SICI

O Carthage

AFRICA

The map shows the extent of the Roman Empire which, by 63BC, encorporated the whole of the Jewish nation.

Emperor Caesar Augustus. He built a port on the coast of Palestine and named it Caesarea. He tried to persuade the Jews to adopt Roman ways, and built a theatre in Jerusalem.

Herod knew that the Jews disliked him and built several strongholds around Palestine, where he could be safe from attack. He was suspicious even of his own family, and executed three of his sons whom he thought were plotting against him. His winter palace by the Dead Sea, Massada, is on a rock three hundred metres high, and can be approached only by one steep path.

This flamingo is one of several mosaics in Caesarea.

The Dead Sea Scrolls

The Dead Sea is the lowest place on earth, four hundred metres lower than the level of other seas in the world. The River Jordan flows into the Dead Sea but nothing flows out. The water just evaporates in the heat, leaving salt behind. Nothing grows. No birds fly.

In 1946, at Qumran on the shore of the Dead Sea, a young shepherd threw a stone into a deserted cave in the cliffs and heard a pottery jar break. The jar contained a scroll of parchment with writing on it. More scrolls were discovered nearby and the remains of buildings where the scrolls had been written.

The scrolls showed that there had been a group of about two hundred men living in this desert. Their leader was called "the Teacher of Justice" and they studied the Bible every day. Many copies of biblical books have been found there, and even the pens with which the scribes wrote them. They expected God to send them a messenger who would make the world a better place. They expected God's messenger to appear and lead the good "sons of light" to destroy the wicked "sons of darkness".

They had a strict rule of life. Anyone who wanted to join the group had to have a trial period before becoming a full member. They shared everything, and no one had personal belongings. Every evening they washed themselves and had supper together. There was always an empty place laid for God's messenger, in the hope that he would come.

When the Roman army was advancing down the Jordan valley to besiege Jerusalem in 68AD, the Roman soldiers destroyed this little community. The men began to hide their texts wrapped in linen and sealed in jars. Finally they rushed to dump them unprotected in hiding places near their settlement, these texts have survived only in fragments.

Inside Cave 4 at Qumran which contained scrolls left by the Essenes at the time of the Roman attack in 68AD.

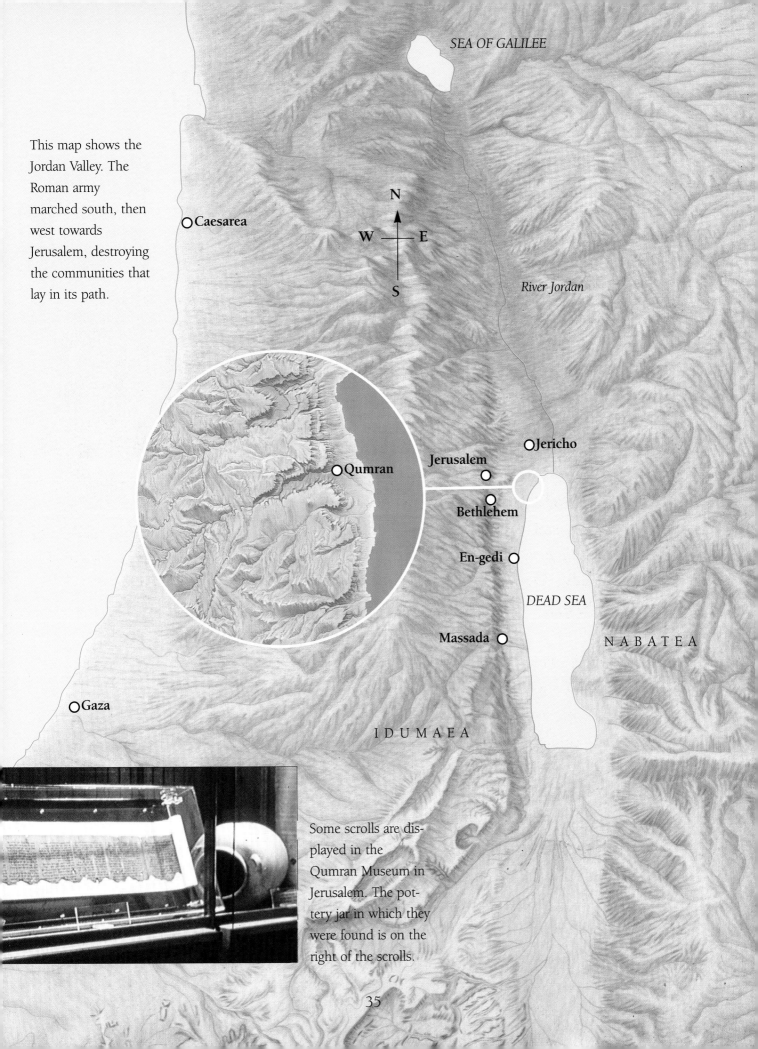

This map shows the Jordan Valley. The Roman army marched south, then west towards Jerusalem, destroying the communities that lay in its path.

SEA OF GALILEE

N
W   E
S

River Jordan

○ Caesarea

○ Qumran

Jericho ○

Jerusalem
○

Bethlehem
○

En-gedi ○

DEAD SEA

Massada ○

NABATEA

○ Gaza

IDUMAEA

Some scrolls are displayed in the Qumran Museum in Jerusalem. The pottery jar in which they were found is on the right of the scrolls.

Jesus in Galilee

When Jesus was about thirty years old he began to teach about the Kingdom of God in Galilee. The Sea of Galilee is still busy with fishermen. Jesus' first disciples were fishermen who lived at Capernaum, a fishing village on the lakeside. Jesus taught them that God's Kingdom was like a net full of fish. Around the lake there was good farmland and Jesus told his followers that God's kingdom was like a seed ripening into rich corn. There was a lot of sickness in those days, and Jesus travelled around healing people.

Modern fishing boats on the Sea of Galilee.

The Romans controlled Galilee. The country was poor because everyone had to pay heavy taxes to Rome. The Romans built roads and some beautiful cities, with grand theatres with decorated mosaic floors. Two of them are Sepphoris, near Jesus' home town of Nazareth, and Tiberius on the lakeside. Jesus never visited them. There were Roman soldiers and officials everywhere. Among them were tax collectors. Nobody liked the tax-collectors, but Jesus chose one to be among his twelve disciples. Matthew was collecting taxes from travellers at the frontier when Jesus called him to be one of his disciples.

Jairus was an official of the synagogue at Capernaum. When he thought his daughter was dying he asked Jesus to help.

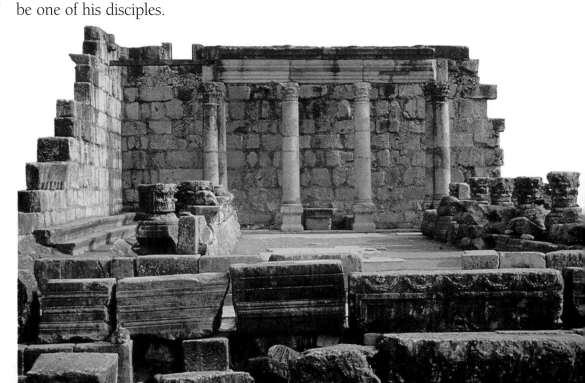

The ruins of the synagogue at Capernaum.

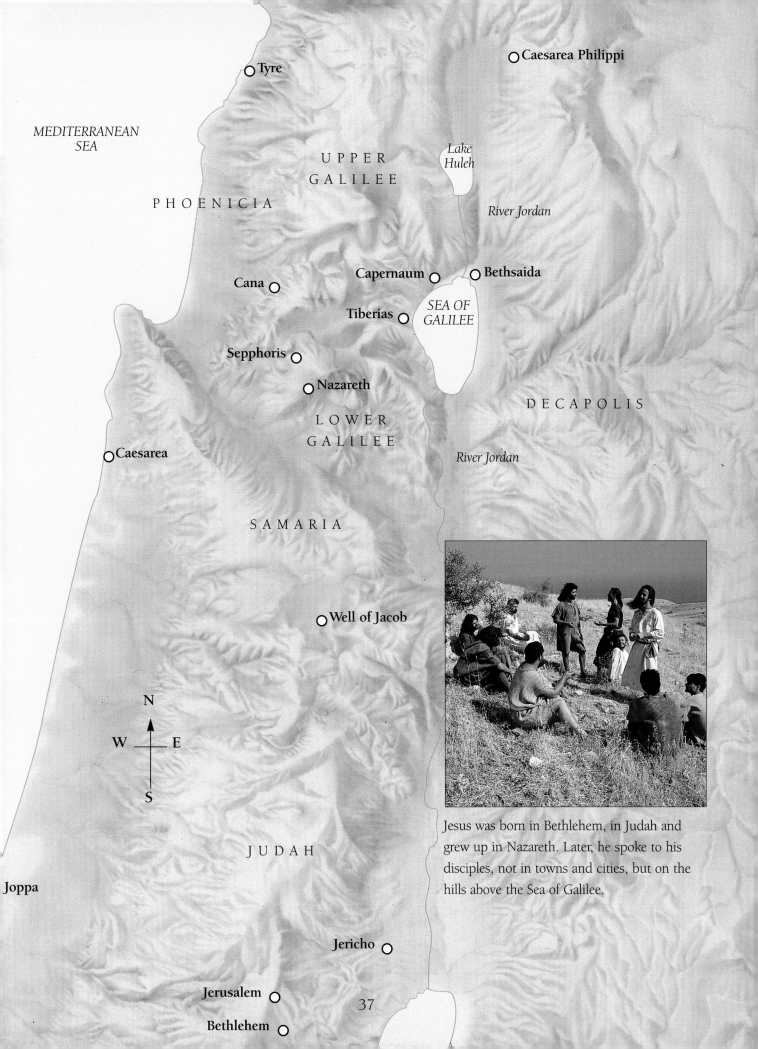

MEDITERRANEAN
SEA

○ Caesarea Philippi

○ Tyre

Lake Huleh

UPPER
GALILEE

PHOENICIA

River Jordan

Cana ○

Capernaum ○ ● Bethsaida

Tiberias ○

SEA OF
GALILEE

Sepphoris ○

○ Nazareth

DECAPOLIS

LOWER
GALILEE

○ Caesarea

River Jordan

SAMARIA

N

W ✛ E

S

Well of Jacob ○

Jesus was born in Bethlehem, in Judah and
grew up in Nazareth. Later, he spoke to his
disciples, not in towns and cities, but on the
hills above the Sea of Galilee.

JUDAH

Joppa

Jericho ○

Jerusalem ○

Bethlehem ○

Jesus in Jerusalem

King Herod built a huge Temple in Jerusalem. He also built many other fine buildings of Roman design including a racecourse. Jerusalem was the finest and most important city in the eastern Roman empire. Herod died about 4BC. His three sons were bad rulers and by 39AD all three had lost their kingdoms to Roman governors.

It was the ambition of every faithful Jew to get to Jerusalem. Pilgrims journeyed for weeks along dusty roads to come and pray in the Temple, especially during the big religious festivals. In the Temple only coins made in Tyre were accepted, so all other coins had first to be changed into Tyrian coins. It was difficult for pilgrims to bring animals for sacrifice with them, so they bought these in the Temple. The high priest ruled the Temple, but during the great feasts the Roman governor of the whole Roman Province also came to Jerusalem from his capital, Caesarea. He brought extra troops to make sure that there was no rioting.

Jesus walked from Galilee for seven days with his twelve disciples for the Passover celebrations in Jerusalem. He proclaimed that God had rejected the Temple and its priesthood, the money changers and birdsellers. The high priest could not accept this. He had Jesus arrested in the Garden of Gethsemane and handed over to the Roman governor, Pontius Pilate. Jesus realised this

Pilgrims travelled from cities many hundreds of miles away to Jerusalem for the Passover festival. It took Jesus over a week to walk there from Galilee

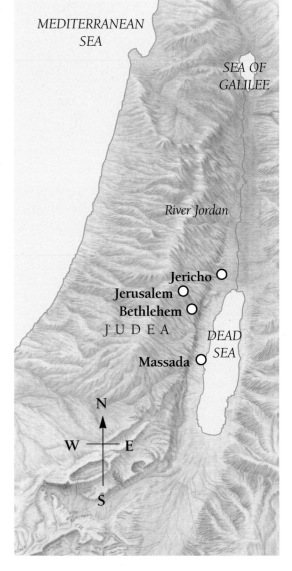

MEDITERRANEAN SEA

SEA OF GALILEE

River Jordan

Jericho ○

Jerusalem ○

Bethlehem ○

J U D E A

DEAD SEA

Massada ○

N
W — E
S

would happen, but did not run away. Pontius Pilate had Jesus tortured and condemned him to death. He was crucified between two thieves, who had also been condemned to be executed, outside the city walls.

Jesus was tortured by Roman soldiers. He was mocked and clothed in a red military cloak and a crown of thorns as if he was a king.

Jesus was crucified between two criminals at Golgotha, which means the place the skull.

A model of Herodian Jerusalem. In the Gospel of Luke, when Jesus approached Jerusalem for the last time, he wept over it and said, "If only you had known the way to peace!"

Paul's Journeys

In the Roman empire travelling was hard work. The easiest way to travel was by sea. But ships were small and were often wrecked by storms, especially in winter. On the land the Roman legions had built stone roads connecting all regions of the empire to Rome. Many are still in use today. Only the rich or official messengers would ride horses or drive chariots. Paul walked thousands of miles along these roads. For ten years he was constantly travelling, spreading the teachings of Jesus.

There were many Jewish communities around the Mediterranean, especially in important cities like Ephesus, Corinth and Rome. They had their own synagogues and a Jewish traveller could expect to be welcomed by other Jews. So Paul first sought out these groups and explained to them about Jesus. He told them that Jesus was the Saviour promised by God. Some accepted this message, but others did not believe him. Often they mocked him or imprisoned

Paul sailed for Rome in winter when the sea was dangerous. The boat sank off Malta, Paul was among those who managed to swim ashore.

This map shows the four journeys Paul made to teach people about Christianity after Jesus' death.

Carthage ○

	First journey
	Second journey
	Third journey
	Last journey

him or drove him away. So he took the message to others who were not Jews. Wherever he left groups of Christians he kept in touch by writing them letters.

In the end his enemies tried to kill him and he was taken prisoner. He appealed to the Roman emperor and he was eventually taken to Rome. On the way he was shipwrecked off Malta. In Rome he spent two years under guard. In 64AD there was a great fire in Rome, which destroyed many people's houses. The Emperor Nero blamed the fire on the Christians and started a brutal persecution against them. Paul may have been beheaded in this persecution.

Paul was kept chained and under guard in Rome for two years, but he continued to preach and write letters.

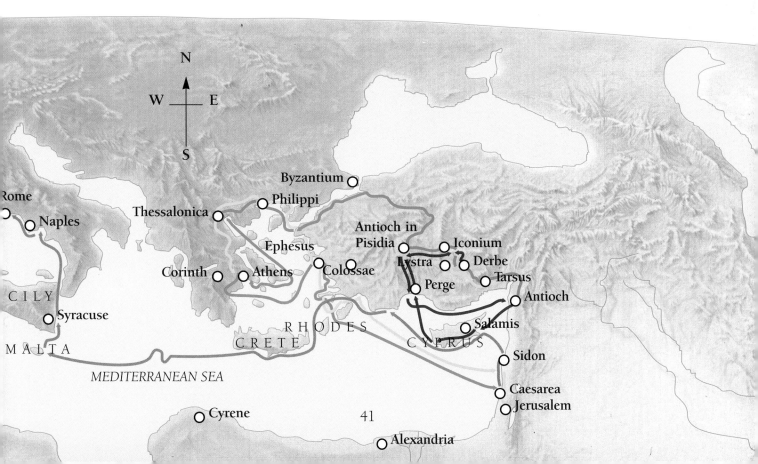

41

The Books of the Old Testament

At first these stories were passed down orally. Later most of them were written down and put into their present order around 400BC.

The Pentateuch
The first five books

Genesis
The stories of the Creation are followed by stories of the patriarchs Abraham, Isaac and Jacob. The book ends with the Hebrews settling in Egypt.

Exodus
The stories of the escape from Egypt. The covenants made between God and his people on Mt Sinai. Laws and customs laid down for their way of life.

Leviticus
The laws for sacrifice and worship in the Temple.

Numbers
Continues the stories of Exodus up to the entry into the Promised Land.

Deuteronomy
The second version of the Law. Found in the Temple in 622 BC it appears as Moses' final instructions.

The Histories
Contains six books of the history of Israel from the entry into the Promised Land until the destruction of Jerusalem.

Joshua
The story of the entry into Canaan under Joshua.

Judges
Events in Canaan under the leaders of Israel, the Judges, until the first kings of Israel and Judah.

Samuel 1 & 2
From Samuel to the death of King David.

Kings 1 & 2
From King Solomon to the sacking of Jerusalem.

The Prophets
The stories about, and the sayings of, the prophets

The prophets were the religious leaders of Israel under the kings. The four great prophets come first in the Bible, followed by the 12 little prophets (this refers to the quantity of their writing).

Isaiah
Started in Jerusalem c. 740BC. The others continued his message.

Jeremiah
Taught during the last years of the kingdom in Jerusalem. c. 627BC.

Ezekiel
Encouraged the exiles in Babylon to keep going c. 590BC.

Daniel
Written in 167BC to encourage the Jews during their persecution by Antiochus.

The Twelve Little Prophets
Hosea, Joel, Amos, Obadiah, Jonah, Micah, Nahum, Habbakuk, Zephaniah, Haggai, Zechariah and Malachi the last of the prophets.

The Writings
A collection of the other books of Hebrew scripture.

The Psalms
The prayer book of Israel.

Proverbs
A collection of wise sayings for living a good life.

Job
A good man who loses everything but his faith and is rewarded by God at the end.

The Song of Songs
A collection of love songs many of which are about the love of God for his people.

Ruth
A short story about the great-grandmother of King David.

Lamentations
A collection of sad songs about the destruction of Jerusalem.

Ecclesiastices
A book discussing if there is a meaning to life.

Esther
The story of a Jewish queen in the Babylonian court, and the delivery of the Jews from persecution.

Ezra and Nehemiah
A pair of books describing the return of the Jews from Babylon.

Chronicles 1 and 2
A history focused on the worship in the Temple.

The Greek Bible
Besides the books written in Hebrew, the Greek Bible contains other books accepted by Greek-speaking Jews and the first Christians. Some Christians do not accept them.

Judith
A Jewish heroine who saved her people by beheading the attacking general.

Tobit
A faithful Jew in exile in Babylon who recovered his sight and a fortune with the help of an angel.

Maccabees 1 and 2
A history of rebellion against King Antiochus in 167BC.

Wisdom
Written in Alexandria in c. 50BC. It contrasts the piety of the Jews and the idolatry of the Egyptians.

Ecclesiasticus
A book of wise sayings.

Baruch
A collection of prayers written after the sacking of Jerusalem.

The Books of the New Testament

The Four Gospels
In the Christian Bible the books of the New Testament are not printed in the order in which they were written. The Gospels were given first place although they were probably written after the Letters of Paul.

The Gospel according to Mark
The shortest of the gospels it records the wonderful personality of Jesus, his suffering and death. Mark's Gospel was written in rough Greek, the sort of language used by slaves, probably in about AD65.

The Gospel according to Matthew
This is especially linked to Matthew the tax collector at Capernaum. It shows that Jesus fulfils the hopes of the Jews for a Messiah. The writer had read Mark's Gospel but included a lot about Jesus' teaching, based on a text of Jesus' sayings. It was possibly written in AD80.

The Gospel according to Luke
This writer had read Mark's Gospel and the same book of sayings of Jesus that was also used by Matthew. It is written in correct Greek for a prosperous audience. Luke may have been a friend of Paul. The same author also wrote a second book. **The Acts of the Apostles,** about how Christianity spread through Palestine, Greece and Rome. Both books were written in about AD85.

The Gospel according to John
This gospel is quite different from the other three. It uses fewer but longer stories about Jesus. It is full of symbols, Jesus calls himself the 'light of the world'. The gospel is based on the witness of the beloved disciple, who is perhaps John, one of Jesus' first companions. It may have been written after his death by his disciples.

The Letters of Paul
These are printed in the Bible according to their length, so the longest letters come first. The apostle Paul wrote them between AD51 and AD62 to encourage, and advise the earliest Christian groups and communities.

Early Letters

Thessalonians 1 and 2
These were a Christian group in Greece which Paul visited at least twice.

The Four "Great" Letters
Galatians were Jewish Christians in central Turkey trying to keep Jewish customs. Paul wrote that Christ had made the old Jewish customs pointless.

Romans
There was a large group of Christians in Rome. Paul explains how Christianity completes Judaism.

Corinthians 1 and 2
These were letters written to the Christians in this large Greek port. Paul wrote to settle disputes among them and explained Christian love to them.

The Letters from Captivity
These were written by Paul from prison in Caesarea and Rome. The letter to the Philippians is especially friendly, and is written to his favourite Christian group in Greece.

Colossians
This was a group of Christians at Colossae in Turkey. Paul explained how Christ was supreme.

Ephesians
This was a similar letter to the Colossians. It stresses that Christians must be united.

Philemon
A short letter to a friend sending back to him a slave who had run away to Paul.

The "Pastoral" letters
Letters written to the pastors in the Church.

Timothy 1 and 2
These letters were written to Paul's disciple, Timothy.

Titus
A letter to Paul's disciple Titus.

The General Letters
The remaining letters of the New Testament are not written to specific groups of people. They were thought to be written by the apostles but scholars doubt that this is correct.

The Letter to the Hebrews
This is *a letter written to Christian converts from Judaism.*

The Letter of James
This is thought by some to be the earliest writing of the New Testament from about AD50. It speaks of the rich and poor.

Three Letters of John
The first long letter is concerned with Christian love. The other two are short.

Two Letters of Peter
The first is a guide to newly-baptised Christians. The second is probably the latest writing in the New Testament.

The Letter of Jude
This is a short letter for Christian converts from Judaism.

The Book of Revelation
This is a series of visions described by John, the gospel writer and is the last book of the New Testament. It tells persecuted Christians that God will look after them and reward them in the end. It describes the final battle between good and evil.

Index of Places